2

D1521375

Activate Your Smile

Discover how the impact of a simple smile can revolutionize your personal and professional life.

Janet Yvette Mitchell

ISBN: 979-8-8764-3026-7

DEDICATION

To my parents in heaven

To my siblings Yoyo, Adriana and Jaime

To my nieces and nephews and to Rocío

JANET Y. MITCHELL

JANET Y. MITCHELL

CONTENTS

ACKNOWLEDGEMENTS

To God for giving me the opportunity to enjoy my profession, helping and serving my patients who have been my inspiration for creating this work.

ACTIVATE YOUR SMILE

INTRODUCTION

"Activate Your Smile" by Janet Yvette Mitchell is a deep and revealing exploration of one of the most universal and powerful human gestures: the smile. Through this book, Dr. Mitchell takes us on a journey that spans from ancient history to modern science, showing how a simple smile can transform our personal and professional lives.

This book, now available to an English-speaking audience, mirrors the journey and insights of its Spanish counterpart, inviting readers across the globe to discover the transformative power of a smile.

With an approach that integrates psychology, neuroscience, and personal experience, the book offers a rich and nuanced perspective on how the smile affects our self-esteem, our social interactions, and our mental and emotional health.

By reading "Activate Your Smile" you will discover no only the importance of smiling but also how to cultivate ar authentic and meaningful smile for your everyday life overcoming challenges and finding a source of joy anc connection with others.

.

Chapter 1

History and Evolution of the Smile: A Journey Through Time

" You never know who might be in love with your smile."
Gabriel García Márquez

In the human journey, the smile has been much more than just a facial expression. This chapter takes us on a journey through the centuries to explore how the smile has evolved, becoming a powerful tool for self-expression, confidence, and self-esteem. From ancient civilizations to our era, we will see how the smile has influenced culture, art and psychology, shaping the way we perceive ourselves and relate to others.

The Smile in Antiquity

The smile, one of the most universal and powerful human expressions, has a rich history intertwined with the evolution of humanity itself. From its origins in the earliest civilizations to its role in contemporary society, the smile has been a constant reflection of culture, emotion, and human communication.

In ancient civilizations, the smile was a symbol of power and divinity. In Egypt, for example, the smile was a symbol of immortality, captured in their monuments and art. Deities were often depicted with serene, smiling expressions, symbolizing benevolence and divine omnipotence. This representation of the smile demonstrates a deep understanding of its emotional impact and symbolic value.

The smile also played a crucial role in ancient Greek and Roman cultures. Philosophers and artists of these times explored the smile in their works, debating its meaning and role in human expression. For the Greeks, the smile was often a reflection of internal happiness and harmony. They considered the smile a gift from the gods, a sign of benevolence and grace. In Rome, it was more associated with cunning and seduction.

These ancestral perceptions teach us that the smile has always been an integral element of the human experience, not just as an expression of joy, but also as a manifestation of well-being and internal balance.

These cultures intuitively understood what today's science confirms: the smile has an intrinsic power to influence our emotional state and our social interactions. By smiling, we not only express happiness, but we also connect with a legacy of positivity and well-being that transcends time.

The Smile Through the History of Art

Art throughout the centuries has captured the essence of the smile in several ways. From Leonardo da Vinci's Mona Lisa, with her enigmatic smile that has captivated the world, to the joyful and lively representations in the works of the Impressionists, the smile has been a recurring theme in art. These representations not only capture moments of joy but also evoke confidence, mystery, and a deep emotional introspection.

The smile in art has served as a mirror of the human condition, reflecting not just states of happiness, but also of reflection, serenity, and sometimes melancholy. This shows how the smile can be a powerful tool of non-verbal communication, capable of conveying a wide spectrum of emotions and moods.

The Smile in Contemporary Society

In modern society, the smile continues to be a vital tool for social interaction and emotional well-being. The 20th century brought significant changes in the perception of the smile. With the rise of psychology and behavioral science, the smile began to be studied as an emotional and social phenomenon. This period saw a growing interest in understanding the smile not just as an expression of happiness but also as a complex tool for non-verbal communication.

The advent of photography and, later, cinema, further transformed our relationship with the smile. These media allowed for capturing and sharing moments of happiness, making the smile a universal symbol of joy and positivity. The smile on the big screen and in photographs became an iconic element of popular culture.

In the 21st century, the smile continues to evolve with technology and social media. The way we smile, how our smile is perceived, and its impact on others are influenced by the omnipresence of cameras and digital platforms. The smile has acquired new dimensions in this digital environment, where it is shared and interpreted through screens.

Despite the changes over the centuries, the smile has maintained its essence as a powerful medium of human connection. Throughout history, the smile has been a mirror of human emotions, reflecting joy, sadness, irony, and love.

Throughout history, the smile has been a faithful reflection of the cultural, social, and emotional evolution of humanity. It has symbolized power, been an object of suspicion, and embodied joy and human wit. This journey through time shows us how a simple expression can have multiple meanings and how these meanings can transform and adapt to changing contexts.

As we close this chapter on the history of the smile, we enter into equally fascinating new territory: "The Science of the Smile." Here we will explore how recent advancements in psychology, neuroscience, and biology have begun to unravel the mysteries behind this very human expression, revealing not only how we smile but why we do it and the profound impact it has on us and those around us.

This next chapter invites us to discover the smile not only as a cultural and historical phenomenon but also as an intriguing and complex biological and emotional process.

Chapter 2

The Science of the Smile

"A smile costs less than electricity and gives more light."
Scottish Proverb

The smile, that simple curvature of the lips, hides behind it a world of complexity and wonder. Since time immemorial, it has been an integral part of the human experience, a universal language that transcends cultures and generations. It's more than a mere reaction to joy; it is a phenomenon deeply rooted in our biology and psychology.

Studies have revealed that even before birth, fetuses can smile within the womb. This fascinating revelation, made possible by ultrasound technology, suggests that the smile is an innate and fundamental expression of the human being. Moreover, children who are born blind also smile, indicating that this expression is not learned solely through imitation, but is part of our nature.

Exploring the smile from a biological standpoint, we find that it is governed by an orchestra of reactions in our brain. When we smile, specific brain regions are activated, such as the prefrontal temporal cortex, the basal ganglia, and the hypothalamus, all areas associated with well-being. This genuine smile, known as the "Duchenne smile", is not only a response to happiness but also a catalyst for it.

It is called the Duchenne smile in honor of the French neurologist Guillaume Duchenne, who in the 19th century was the first to study and describe the difference between a genuine smile and a forced smile. Duchenne identified that authentic smiles involve not only the muscles of the mouth but also the muscles around the eyes.

Smiling stimulates the release of neurotransmitters like dopamine, serotonin, and endorphins, which make us feel good, and at the same time, it reduces the levels of cortisol, the hormone related to stress. Dopamine is known as the "pleasure chemical," playing a crucial role in how we experience pleasure and satisfaction. Serotonin, on the other hand, regulates mood, happiness, and anxiety. Endorphins are our natural painkillers, helping us to alleviate pain and stress. Simultaneously, smiling reduces cortisol levels, the stress hormone, helping us to relax and feel calmer.

The smile involves different facial muscles depending on its intensity (see Appendix). In subtle smiles, around 12 muscles are activated, while in broad and genuine smiles, like the "Duchenne smile," up to 17 muscles are activated. Among these muscles are the zygomatic major and minor, the orbicularis oculi, and the levator anguli oris. This activation not only creates the smile's expression but also sends signals to the brain that promote emotional well-being.

Interestingly, frowning, often an expression of negative emotions, involves several muscles similar to a subtle smile. This indicates that, in terms of muscular effort, it might be as easy to frown as it is to smile. However, the emotional effects of smiling are significantly more positive.

But the smile doesn't only affect the one who offers it; its power extends to those who receive it. Studies have shown that smiling, even when not feeling naturally happy, can have beneficial effects on mental and physical health, both for oneself and for others. This ability of the smile to improve interpersonal relationships and convey friendliness, trust, and openness is a powerful tool in our daily interactions.

Smiling has a profound effect on our mood and overall well-being. This action, even when forced, can trick the brain into releasing neurotransmitters associated with happiness, like dopamine and serotonin. This release not only improves our sense of happiness but can also reduce cortisol levels, the stress hormone.

Scientific research has gone further, exploring how smiling influences stress situations. An experiment at the University of Kansas showed that smiling during stressful tasks can lead to a quicker recovery from stress, demonstrating that maintaining positive facial expressions, even in difficult moments, has physiological and psychological benefits. This ability of the smile to mitigate stress and enhance emotional recovery is a window into understanding its therapeutic power.

In the customer service field, smiling plays a crucial role, as demonstrated in the groundbreaking study by Tobias Otterbring, "Smile for a while: the effect of employee-displayed smiling on customer affect and satisfaction" from 2017. This study, the first of its kind to experimentally examine the isolated impact of employee smiles on customers' emotional states and satisfaction, reveals significant results. Otterbring found that employees who smile not only improve customer satisfaction but also positively influence their emotional states.

Based on the stimulus-organism-response framework and theories of emotional contagion, the study emphasizes that a smiling employee increases customer satisfaction primarily through pleasure. This study reinforces the importance of the smile in creating positive and satisfying customer experiences, highlighting that a simple smile can be a powerful tool to enhance customer interaction and perception in service environments.

Exploring the science behind the first impression reveals a fascinating game of perceptions that occur in the blink of an eye. Various studies agree that it only takes about 7 seconds to form a first impression of someone we just met. In this brief period, our brain quickly evaluates key aspects like appearance, behavior, and communication of the other. This process, though ephemeral, lays the foundation for how we will be perceived in future interactions.

The smile, in this context, plays a crucial role, as it conveys openness, accessibility, and trust, essential characteristics for leaving a positive and lasting impression. In the professional realm, where each encounter can open doors to new opportunities, understanding and adequately managing these first moments is vital.

Finally, the smile is a bridge to empathy. Thanks to mirror neurons, when we see someone smile, we feel the impulse to replicate that expression, creating a bond of understanding and emotional connection. This contagion of smiles not only improves our social interactions but also reinforces our capacity to relate to and understand others.

As we close this chapter on the science of the smile, we delve into an even more personal terrain: the smile and self-esteem. How can this facial expression influence our own perception and our confidence? The next chapter will unveil how the smile can be a powerful tool to transform our self-image and strengthen our emotional well-being.

Chapter 3

Smile and Self-Esteem

"The smile is the reflection of the soul."
Anonymous

The smile, that expression which we've discovered to have deep roots in our biology, is intimately intertwined with our self-esteem. Self-esteem, the concept that defines how we value and trust in our abilities, is influenced not just by what we think, but also by how we express ourselves. In this chapter, we explore how the smile acts as a reflection and reinforcement of our internal image, playing a vital role in building healthy self-esteem.

The smile goes beyond being an indicator of happiness; it's a catalyst for feeling good about ourselves. When we smile, we send ourselves a powerful message of self acceptance and positivity. This simple action can change the way we view ourselves, helping us to perceive a more joyful and confident version of ourselves.

Here's where science offers a fascinating perspective; when we smile, areas in our brain associated with reward and emotional well-being are activated, which in turn can improve our self-worth and confidence perception.

But the smile doesn't just affect us internally; it also has a profound impact on how we relate to the world. When we smile, we are perceived as more approachable and friendly, which improves our social interactions. These positive relationships, in turn, reinforce our self-esteem, creating a virtuous circle of positive feedback. Being seen as more open and trustworthy not only improves our current relationships but also opens doors to new friendships and connections.

Incorporating smiling into our daily life can be an effective strategy for nurturing our self-esteem. From smiling at the mirror as an act of self-affirmation each morning to recalling and reliving happy moments throughout the day, these simple yet powerful practices can make a significant difference in how we feel about ourselves. Additionally, adopting a body posture that reflects confidence and joy can reinforce this effect, creating a body language that communicates and reinforces self-acceptance and self-worth.

The smile, in its authenticity and simplicity, is a tool for self-acceptance. Accepting and loving ourselves as we are, with all our strengths and weaknesses, is essential for solid self-esteem. The smile invites us to embrace our identity, to value ourselves, and to project that self-esteem outwardly.

The influence of the smile on others' perception of us and how this affects our self-esteem is backed by scientific research. A study conducted by the University of South Australia highlights how the smile can trick our mind into perceiving stimuli more positively. Participants who adopted a forced smile facial position by holding a pen between their teeth tended to interpret others' facial expressions and body movements as more positive compared to those who did not. This suggests that activating a smile contributes to a positive neurological reaction, making us, when our facial muscles indicate happiness, tend to experience the world in a more positive way.

Another study, published in "Scientific Reports," investigated self-perception of smile attractiveness. This study found that certain dimensions of the smile, like the proportional width of the smile, have a significant impact on self-perception of smile attractiveness. For every 10% increase in the proportional width of the smile, self-perceived attractiveness increased proportionally. While gender did not appear to affect self-perception of smile attractiveness, dimensions of the smile did show a significant association. This finding indicates that the way we perceive our own smile can influence how we feel about ourselves.

These studies reinforce the idea that the smile not only reflects our internal emotional state but can also influence how we perceive ourselves and how others perceive us. A smile perceived as attractive can improve our self-esteem and social interactions, which in turn can reinforce a positive perception of ourselves.

In summary, the smile acts as a bidirectional mirror, reflecting and affecting both our self-image and the image we project to others. As we conclude this chapter, we've discovered how the smile can be an invaluable ally in our quest for stronger, healthier self-esteem.

In the next chapter, we explore a unique emotional journey that we've all shared. Discover how masks, which became a shield during the pandemic, affected our self-esteem and our smiles. Dive into this article to find a blend of psychology, shared experiences, and the challenge of rediscovering our smiles in the post-pandemic era.

Chapter 4

The Smile During the Pandemic: Hidden Smiles and Self-Esteem

"Beauty is power, a smile is its sword."
Anonymous

The COVID-19 pandemic drastically changed our way of life, introducing not only health challenges but also psychological ones. One of the most notable changes was the widespread use of masks, which had an unexpected impact on many people's self-esteem. This article explores how the act of hiding our smile behind masks affected our self-image and what happens now as we return to a world where smiles are again visible.

The Impact of the Pandemic and the Return to Normality

At the beginning of the pandemic, masks became a symbol of caution and safety. However, they also concealed one of our most fundamental tools of expression: the smile. For many, this had a paradoxical effect on self-esteem, offering a veil of security by hiding physical insecurities, such as the appearance of teeth or the way of smiling.

The mask provided an unexpected refuge for some people. Those who used to feel insecure about their smile found comfort in hiding it. This phenomenon suggests a complex relationship between our facial expression and our self-perception.

Psychologists and behavioral experts noticed significant changes in how we interact socially with the use of masks. The lack of visible facial expressions, especially smiles, affected the way we perceived and connected with others, leading to a greater reliance on non-verbal communication and body language.

With the gradual lifting of restrictions and less use of masks, many people face a new challenge: showing their smile again. This change has rekindled old insecurities for some, who during the pandemic got used to hiding part of their face.

The COVID-19 pandemic has profoundly impacted our way of communicating and expressing emotions. There are articles highlighting the need for smile classes, designed to help us reconnect with this fundamental facial expression.

These classes aim not only to regain the physical ability t smile but also to restore the emotional and social connectio that was lost by hiding our smiles behind masks.

In this context, learning to smile again becomes an ac of reconciliation with ourselves and society, recognizing th smile as a bridge to empathy and mutual understanding in world emerging from adversity.

The return to normality presents an opportunity t confront and overcome insecurities related to smiling Mental health professionals suggest that this is an ideal tim to work on self-acceptance and self-confidence.

The pandemic forced us to cover our smiles, but it als gave us a unique perspective on the importance of thi expression in our daily lives. Now that we are returning to : reality where our smiles are again visible, we face th challenge of reconciling our self-image with the ope expression of our emotions. This process is an opportunit to grow in confidence and self-acceptance.

Looking forward, the next chapter will focus on a particularly important group: teenagers. We will explore how the smile can be a transformative tool for them, helping them navigate challenges like bullying and social anxiety, and how it can become a valuable resource in this crucial stage of their lives.

Chapter 5

The Smile in Adolescence

"Smile, it's the key that fits the lock of everyone's heart."
Anthony J. D'Angelo

Adolescence is a stage of transformation and growth where the smile and self-esteem can be challenged by a variety of factors. This chapter delves into the crucial role the smile plays during these formative years, exploring how physical changes, such as dental turnover and acne, as well as parental support in these areas, can influence teenagers confidence and willingness to smile.

During this stage, young people experience significan changes. The transition from baby teeth to permanent teeth can be a source of concern for many, especially if they face issues like misaligned or crowded teeth. Added to this is the challenge of acne, a common condition that can deeply affect self-image. These aesthetic insecurities can make adolescents hesitant about their smile and their appearance in general.

In this context, the role of parents and guardians is fundamental. Subtle but effective support, such as providing proper dental care or seeking treatment for acne, can make

ۥ significant difference. This type of care not only helps to resolve aesthetic issues but also conveys a message of support and understanding to teenagers, reinforcing their self-esteem, and encouraging them to smile confidently.

Social pressure in adolescence is intense, and the desire to fit in and be accepted becomes a priority. In this scenario, insecurities about appearance can make adolescents hide their smile. Promoting an environment of acceptance and empathy, where authenticity is valued more than physical perfection, is essential to help them feel secure and comfortable in expressing their joy.

Bullying, whether in person or online, can leave deep emotional scars. Supporting teenagers to face these situations with resilience and helping them find their inner strength can be key to them regaining their smile. In these cases, the smile is not a denial of problems but a reflection of strength and the ability to overcome challenges.

Amidst family issues and academic pressure, finding reasons to smile can be challenging. Here, small actions and the constant support of parents can be very helpful, reminding them that there are reasons to smile even i difficult times.

Encouraging activities that generate joy, laughter, an creative expression can be a useful tool to help teenager integrate smiling into their daily life. Teaching them tha authenticity is more important than maintaining a facade o constant happiness is vital for their emotional developmen

We've covered how the smile can be a source o strength and confidence for teenagers, especially wit parental support in dental, facial, and emotional aspects. I the next chapter, we'll see how the smile can influence th professional world, particularly in areas of sales an customer service, where trust and positivity play an essentia role in success.

Chapter 6

The Smile in the Professional World

"The smile is the universal language of kindness."
William Arthur Ward

In the professional world, especially in areas such as sales and customer service, the smile becomes a crucial element for success. A genuine smile can positively impact professional performance and the building of lasting relationships with customers.

The smile is not just an expression of joy but a powerful tool in non-verbal communication. By smiling, we not only show a friendly and approachable facet, but we also enhance the positive perception of those around us. In the first few seconds of an encounter, a genuine smile can be the decisive factor that tips the balance in our favor, creating an atmosphere of trust and empathy.

In the workplace, where first impressions can be so determining, cultivating an authentic smile and knowing how to use it strategically becomes an invaluable skill. By integrating this knowledge into our daily life, we not only improve our interpersonal relationships but also pave the way to personal and professional success.

A smile not only creates a positive first impression but also "breaks the ice," establishing common ground and an atmosphere of cordiality from the beginning. This is especially important in sales and customer service, where a smile can be the first step in building a trusting and close relationship with the customer.

In the purchasing process, a customer who has had a positive experience, marked by warm and efficient service, is more likely to return not only for the product but also for the service received. Here, the smile plays a vital role in creating a memorable experience for the customer, strengthening the company's image, and fostering customer loyalty.

According to a 2012 study by Kim and Yoon, analyzing interactions in a clothing store in Seoul, it was observed that employees who smiled positively favorably influenced customer behavior, generating an atmosphere of mutual satisfaction, suggesting that the smile can be a powerful tool to enhance the customer experience and boost sales.

In an innovative experiment conducted by researchers at the University of Oxford in 2001, the power of the smile to foster an open and cooperative attitude was demonstrated. In this study, smiling photographs were shown to participants before a game, resulting in a greater willingness to collaborate and a positive perception of the partner. This underscores the idea that a smile is perceived as a sign of cooperation and can establish a solid foundation for successful professional relationships.

In the workplace, a sincere smile also improves the work environment, fostering a culture of collaboration and support among colleagues. Additionally, in negotiation situations or conflict resolution, a smile can help to soften tensions, facilitating communication and the search for mutually beneficial solutions.

Furthermore, researchers from the universities of California and Michigan discovered that even subconscious exposure to smiling faces can influence decisions like consumer spending. In their study, people briefly exposed to smiling faces were willing to pay more for a drink compared to those who saw frowning faces. This suggests that the smile, consciously or unconsciously processed, facilitates an open attitude, enhancing sales interactions and improving business outcomes.

However, it's crucial that the smile be authentic. A forced smile can be counterproductive, generating an impression of insincerity. Therefore, cultivating a positive and genuine attitude is essential for the smile to sincerely reflect this disposition.

The smile in the professional world is a powerful tool that, when employed authentically and strategically, can have a significant impact on sales, customer service, and team dynamics. In the next chapter, we will address how to understand and leverage the influence of the smile on your path to effective leadership and entrepreneurial success.

Chapter 7

Leadership and Entrepreneurship:

The Impact of a Smile

"If you see someone without a smile, give them one of yours."
Dolly Parton

In the world of leadership and entrepreneurship, communication skills and the ability to establish solid relationships are essential. In this context, the smile emerges as a powerful, often underestimated tool capable of transforming interactions, facilitating communication, and strengthening bonds.

A genuine smile has the power to open doors in the business world. By smiling, a leader or entrepreneur conveys accessibility and empathy, fundamental qualities for creating a positive and motivating work environment. In meetings, negotiations, or even in daily communication, a smile can ease tensions, facilitate openness, and encourage constructive dialogue.

In leadership, a smile reflects confidence and assurance. A leader who smiles not only demonstrates self-confidence but also a positive attitude towards challenges and the people around them. This attitude is contagious, inspiring an atmosphere of optimism and resilience within the team. Moreover, a sincere smile can be a powerful indicator of honesty and transparency, qualities highly valued in any professional environment.

In the realm of entrepreneurship, the smile becomes a key element for networking and attracting opportunities. An entrepreneur who knows how to strategically use their smile can create a memorable impression, facilitate connections with clients, investors, and collaborators, and stand out in a competitive environment. The smile communicates enthusiasm and passion for the project, crucial elements for attracting and maintaining the interest of others.

The smile also plays a crucial role in conflict management and negotiation. In tense or challenging situations, a smile can act as a natural soother, decreasing hostility and paving the way for constructive solutions. In negotiation, an empathetic smile can help create common ground and foster an atmosphere of collaboration and mutual respect.

Moreover, in the world of entrepreneurship, where failure and challenges are part of the process, the smile becomes an expression of resilience. Maintaining a positive attitude and knowing how to smile in the face of obstacle can be a determining factor for overcoming them and moving forward.

In summary, in the universe of leadership and entrepreneurship, the smile is not just a facial expression. It' a powerful communication tool, a symbol of trust, empathy and resilience, and a catalyst for building solid and lasting relationships. Through a smile, leaders and entrepreneur can positively influence their environment, inspire their teams, and pave the way for success.

As we progress on our journey through "Activate You Smile" we delve into an essential and deeply inspiring chapter: "Overcoming Obstacles to Smile." Here, we'l explore not only the challenges that often prevent us from smiling but also the strategies and tools to overcome them.

This chapter is a reminder that, although life may present difficulties, the ability to smile in the face of them is a powerful force that resides within each of us. Prepare to embark on a transformative journey that will lead you to rediscover the healing and liberating power of a smile.

Chapter 8

Overcoming Obstacles to Smile

"The smile enriches those who receive it, without impoverishing those who give it."
Dale Carnegie

Although the smile is a powerful tool in both personal and professional life, we often encounter obstacles that can prevent us from smiling. This chapter focuses on identifying these challenges and exploring effective ways to overcome them, allowing us to unleash the full potential of our smile.

One of the main obstacles to smiling is stress and anxiety. In a world that moves at a fast pace, stress has become a regular part of daily life. This constant state of tension can make us forget the importance of smiling and how a simple smile can relieve stress. Stress management techniques, such as meditation, regular exercise, and practicing gratitude, can help us find moments of peace and joy in our daily routine, facilitating the natural occurrence of a smile.

Another challenge is self-consciousness or insecurity about our appearance, especially when facing issues like acne in adolescence or dental insecurities. These issues can make some people feel uncomfortable smiling. Here, personal acceptance and recognizing that our smile is an expression of our inner joy and not just our outer appearance can be important steps. In cases where these concerns deeply affect self-esteem, seeking professional advice and support can be a beneficial path.

Depression and other mental health issues can also be significant barriers to smiling. These conditions, which profoundly affect mood and energy, require a compassionate and professional approach. Therapy, support from loved ones, and, in some cases, medical intervention, can be crucial in addressing these conditions and regaining the ability to smile.

In the workplace, a toxic or highly competitive work environment can suppress the natural inclination to smile. In these environments, fostering a culture of support and respect, and looking for ways to improve job satisfaction and work-life balance, can be key steps in regaining joy and smiles at work.

Finally, a lack of authenticity in our relationships and environment can make smiling feel forced or fake. Developing genuine relationships and seeking environment where we can be ourselves will allow us to smile more easily and naturally.

We have identified and explored common obstacles that can prevent us from smiling and ways to overcome them. By facing and addressing these challenges, we can start to smile more freely, tapping into the benefits that a genuine smile can bring to our lives. In the next chapter, we will delve into techniques and practices to cultivate a natural and sincere smile, reflecting our inner well-being and happiness.

Chapter 9

Exercises for a Natural Smile

"A smile is a curve that sets everything straight."
Phyllis Diller

In the journey to activate the power of our smile cultivating a natural and sincere smile is essential fo reflecting our inner well-being. Let's explore specifi techniques and exercises to develop a smile that emanate authenticity and joy.

- The Conscious Smile and Self-Observation

The practice of self-observation and the consciou smile is a fundamental first step. In front of a mirror, w dedicate ourselves to smiling and observing how thi action affects our emotional and physical state. Thi simple but widely recognized technique in exercises o self-awareness helps us connect with our smile an understand its impact on our well-being.

In the context of dental problems, self-awareness about the appearance of the smile can persist even after the dental issues have been resolved.

This can lead to a kind of inhibition in the expression of the smile. The person may feel insecure about how their smile looks now or how it will be received by others. These concerns can make it difficult for them to smile spontaneously or authentically, even after the dental problems have been addressed.

To overcome these challenges, there are several strategies that can be employed. Consulting a health professional is essential to assess the condition and recommend appropriate treatment options. This may include physical therapy, medication, or other interventions. Additionally, practicing facial exercises can help to strengthen the muscles responsible for smiling, facilitating the formation of a natural and confident smile.

If the issue with the smile is related to emotional factors, seeking emotional support can be beneficial. Talking to a therapist or counselor can help address any underlying issues and develop coping strategies to improve emotional well-being.

The difficulty in smiling after resolving dental issues can be a complex challenge encompassing both physical and emotional aspects. Addressing these issues with a comprehensive approach, which includes both physical health care and emotional support, can help individuals regain their ability to smile confidently and joyfully.

- Thich Nhat Hanh's Smile Meditation

Thich Nhat Hanh, a globally renowned Vietnamese Zen master, poet, and peace activist, popularized the smile meditation. It's a mindfulness technique that combines meditation with a gentle smile. This practice helps calm the mind and infuse our being with feelings of joy and serenity, reflecting an internal smile that naturally projects outward.

- Positive Visualization and Affirmations by Louise Hay

Positive visualization combined with positive affirmations, as promoted by Louise Hay, an influential American author, motivational speaker, and leader in the self-help and personal development movement, is a powerful tool in positive psychology. By visualizing joyful experiences and reinforcing them with positive affirmations while smiling in front of the mirror, we strengthen our positive self-image and encourage an attitude of confidence and self-love.

- Gratitude Practices and Positive Psychology

The practice of gratitude, supported by studies from psychologists like Martin Seligman, involves recognizing and appreciating the positive things in our life. At the end of the day, we reflect on three things that made us happy, combining it with a smile in front of the mirror. This practice cultivates a positive attitude and a disposition to smile.

- Exercise, Endorphins, and Well-being

Physical exercise, an effective method for stimulating the release of endorphins, helps promote a more frequent and genuine smile. Activities that we enjoy and make us feel good, such as yoga, dancing, or jogging, are fundamental for maintaining a positive mood and a natural smile.

- Positive Visualization Technique

Positive visualization is a key tool in positive psychology. It involves actively imagining situations or happy memories that make us smile. This regular practice helps us connect with feelings of joy and gratitude, encouraging a more spontaneous smile.

- Smiling Breath Technique

Incorporating the smile into our daily breathing can be transformative. During moments of mindful breathing, we can gently smile, combining the benefits of deep breathing with the joyful sensation that a smile provides. This exercise helps to alleviate stress and increase the feeling of relaxation and contentment.

- The Smile in Communication

Finally, practicing the smile in our daily interactions whether at work, university, with friends, or at home, can strengthen our relationships. A sincere smile during conversations not only improves our communication but also strengthens the bonds with the people around us.

These exercises and techniques offer a range of options for you to find your way to a more natural and sincere smile. By integrating these practices into daily life, we can improve not only our facial expression but also our emotional health and overall well-being. In the next chapter, we will address how to carry this smile with confidence in our daily interactions and challenging situations, strengthening our relationships and presence in the world.

Chapter 10

The Smile in Everyday Life:

Building Relationships and Overcoming Challenges

"A smile is the prettiest makeup any girl can wear."
Marilyn Monroe

This chapter focuses on how to carry the smile we have cultivated into our everyday life, using this powerful tool to enhance our relationships and face daily challenges. Through "Activate your Smile" we have explored how to develop an authentic smile; now, we learn to apply it in various aspects of our life.

The Smile in Personal Relationships

Our personal relationships can greatly benefit from a genuine smile. Smiling not only conveys warmth and openness, but it can also help strengthen bonds with friends, family, classmates, and work colleagues. A sincere smile can be the first step to resolving misunderstandings or softening moments of tension. Additionally, in moments of shared joy, a smile can intensify the connection and empathy between people.

The Smile as a Tool for Resilience

In difficult moments, a smile can be a tool for resilience. Facing challenges or stress, a smile can help maintain a positive attitude, even when circumstances seem overwhelming. This attitude doesn't mean ignoring difficulties, but rather approaching them with a more balanced and hopeful perspective.

The Smile at Work

In the work environment, the smile becomes an essential tool for non-verbal communication. It can improve collaboration among colleagues and create a more positive and productive work atmosphere. Moreover, in roles that involve customer service, a genuine smile can make a difference in the customer experience, leaving a lasting impression of professionalism and warmth.

Overcoming Shyness and Social Anxiety

For those facing shyness or social anxiety, the smile can be a valuable ally. Smiling can make us feel more confident and relaxed in social interactions, breaking down barriers and facilitating communication. The smile can be a bridge to new friendships and social opportunities.

Daily Practices

Integrating the smile into our daily routine involves consciously choosing to smile in different situations, from a casual conversation to an important meeting. We can start each day with a smile, setting a positive tone for whatever comes. Additionally, remembering to smile in moments of gratitude or enjoyment increases our awareness and appreciation of the small joys of life.

This chapter has shown us how a smile, cultivated through self-awareness and practice, can enrich our lives on many levels. By "Activating your Smile" in everyday life, we not only improve our interactions and face challenges with greater optimism, but we also contribute to a more positive and welcoming environment for ourselves and those around us. In the next chapter, we will explore how to maintain a healthy and radiant smile, both inside and out.

Chapter 11

Maintaining a Healthy Smile:

Inner and Outer Care

"Use your smile to change the world,
don't let the world change your smile."
Anonymous

We come to the final chapter of "Activate Your Smile", where we focus on the comprehensive care of our smile. A healthy smile is not just about dental aesthetics but also about the emotional and mental well-being that supports it. This chapter addresses how to care for and maintain our smile, both from the inside and out, so that it genuinely reflects our happiness and confidence.

Dental and Facial Care

Dental care is fundamental for a healthy smile. This includes basic practices such as regular brushing, flossing, and periodic visits to the dentist. Good dental hygiene not only protects our teeth and gums but also gives us the confidence to smile without reservations.

In addition, we now have the possibility of improving smiles with orthodontic treatments, to move and position teeth in the mouth and achieve more harmonious smiles. There are various techniques for this, from classic metal braces to new invisible plastic technologies, known as aligners, which are widely accepted by professional adults.

Besides dental care, facial care also plays a significant role. The skin, especially around the mouth and lips, needs attention to maintain a healthy appearance. This can include hydration, sun protection, and, in some cases, specific treatments for conditions like acne.

Emotional and Mental Well-being

An authentic smile reflects emotional and mental well-being. Maintaining a positive attitude, practicing gratitude, and seeking activities that fill us with joy are essential for cultivating an inner smile. Taking care of our mental health, through practices like meditation, mindfulness, or even therapy, can be crucial for maintaining a genuine smile.

Nutrition and Exercise

Nutrition and exercise also contribute to a health smile. A balanced diet, rich in fruits, vegetables, and essentia nutrients, supports dental and general health. Regula exercise, by releasing endorphins, improves our mood an encourages a more frequent and natural smile.

Social Connection and Laughter

Finally, maintaining healthy social connections an seeking moments to laugh and enjoy with others are vital fo our emotional health and for maintaining a radiant smile Positive relationships and shared moments of laughter ca have a significant impact on our disposition to smile.

In summary, this chapter teaches us that the care of ou smile goes beyond the superficial. A healthy smile reflect comprehensive care that encompasses our dental, emotional, physical, and social health. By "Activating Your Smile" in this holistic way, we not only improve our appearance but also enrich our quality of life and overall well-being.

With this, we close our book, hoping to have provided valuable tools and insights that inspire our readers to lead a happier and more smiling life.

Conclusion

Beyond a Smile:

The Journey Continues

"The smile is the sun that drives away the winter
from the human face."
Victor Hugo

As we conclude "Activate Your Smile", we have embarked on a fascinating journey through the transformative power of a simple smile. From understanding its scientific impact on our brain and emotions to implementing it in our daily and professional lives, this book has sought to provide a comprehensive guide to harnessing the smile as a tool for well-being and personal growth.

Final Reflections

As we have seen, the smile is much more than a facial expression. It's a reflection of our inner world, a manifestation of happiness, confidence, and resilience. By smiling, we not only improve our mental and physical health, but we also enhance our social interactions, strengthen our relationships, and face life's challenges with a more positive attitude.

Recommendations for the Future

Practice Conscious Smiling: Continue with the exercises of conscious smiling and meditation. Make smiling a regular part of your mindfulness practice.

Take Care of Your Dental and Emotional Health: Maintain good dental hygiene and care for your emotional well-being. Remember that a healthy smile is both physical and emotional.

Cultivate Positive Relationships: Surround yourself with people who make you smile. Positive relationships are key to maintaining an authentic smile.

Face Challenges with a Smile: Use the smile as a tool to face challenges. Remember that a positive attitude can change your perspective on problems.

Continue Learning and Growing: The smile is just the beginning of a journey of self-discovery and growth. Keep exploring ways to improve your well-being and happiness.

Farewell

As we close this book, it's important to remember that every smile has a story, an emotion, and a purpose behind it. "Activate Your Smile" is not just a set of techniques and advice; it's an invitation to live a more fulfilling, joyful, and satisfying life. I hope this book has been a valuable companion on your path to happiness and that the smile you've cultivated illuminate not only your days but also those of the people around you.

With every smile you share, you're creating a brighter and more positive world. May your smile always reflect the joy and beauty you carry within.

APPENDIX

The following is a detailed representation of the muscles involved in the act of smiling. This action, though it seems simple, involves several facial muscles working together:

1. Major Zygomatic Muscle: This muscle is one of the main responsible for smiling. It extends from the cheekbone to the corner of the mouth, and when contracted, it elevates the lips upwards and outwards.

2. Minor Zygomatic Muscle: Located just below the major zygomatic, this muscle helps deepen the smile by elevating the upper lip.

3. Risorius Muscle: This muscle pulls the corners of the lips backward and upward, contributing to the expression of the smile.

4. Orbicularis Oris Muscles: Although their main function is to close the lips, they also participate in the

smile by controlling the shape and movement of th
lips.

5. Levator Labii Superioris Alaeque Nasi Muscle: As it
   name suggests, this muscle elevates the upper lip an
   contributes to widening the nose during a smile.

6. Levator Labii Superioris Muscle: Different from th
   previous one, this muscle focuses on elevating th
   upper lip, exposing the upper teeth in a genuine smile

7. Buccinator Muscle: Located in the cheek, this muscl
   helps to tense the cheek against the teeth and
   contributes to the appearance of a narrow smile.

8. Depressor Anguli Oris Muscle: Although its mair
   function is to lower the corners of the mouth, in ;
   smile it acts more subtly to moderate the expression.

9. Orbicularis Oculi Muscle: This muscle surrounds the eye, and while its main function is to close the eyelids, it is also involved in the expression of laughter and smiling.

When we smile, laugh, or squint, this muscle contracts, forming folds in the skin around the eye. Over time and with the repetition of these facial expressions, along with factors such as age, loss of skin elasticity, and sun exposure, these lines can become more permanent, leading to "crow's feet."

It is noteworthy that a smile not only involves the action of these muscles but also coordination with the nervous system, which controls the activation and intensity of the smile. Additionally, there are variations in how each person smiles, due to differences in muscle structure and emotional response.

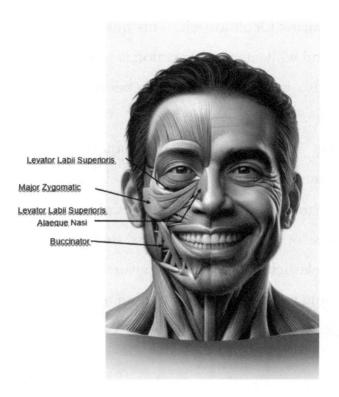

Levator Labii Superioris

Major Zygomatic

Levator Labii Superioris
Alaeque Nasi

Buccinator

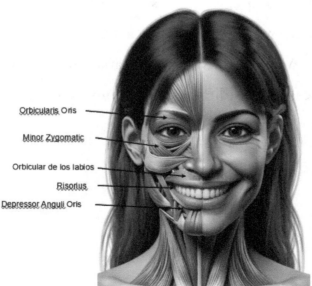

Orbicularis Oris

Minor Zygomatic

Orbicular de los labios

Risorius

Depressor Anguli Oris

BIBLIOGRAPHY

Cross MP, Acevedo AM, Leger KA, Pressman SD. How and why could smiling influence physical health? A conceptual review. Health Psychol Rev. 2023 Jun;17(2):321-343.

DOI: 10.1080/17437199.2022.2052740. Epub 2022 Mar 23. PMID: 35285408.

Horn, S., Matuszewska, N., Gkantidis, N. et al. (2021). Smile dimensions affect self-perceived smile attractiveness. Sci Rep 11, 2779. DOI: 10.1038/s41598-021-82478-9.

Khawaja, A. (2022). El estudio que mostró que los fetos en el vientre "sonríen" cuando sus mamás comen zanahorias y "fruncen el ceño" cuando comen col rizada. Obtained from BBC News Mundo: https://www.bbc.com/mundo/noticias-63016549.

Kim, E., & Yoon, D. J. (2012). Why does service with a smile make employees happy? A social interaction model Journal of Applied Psychology, 97(5), 1059-1067. DOI:10.1037/a0029327.

Kraft, T. L., & Pressman, S. D. (2012). Grin and bear it: the influence of manipulated facial expressions on the stress response. Psychological Science, 23(11), 1372 1378. DOI: 10.1177/0956797612445312.

Otterbring, T. (2017). Smile for a while: the effect o employee-displayed smiling on customer affect and satisfaction. Journal of Service Management, 28(2) 284-304. DOI: 10.1108/JOSM-11-2015-0372.

Prieto, M. D. (2005). La primera impresión. Muestre lo mejor de sí mismo y ¡sonría! Obtained from protocolo.org: https://www.protocolo.org/laboral/imagen-profesional/la-primera-impresion-muestre-lo-mejor-de-si-mismo-y-sonria.html.

Robinson, B. E. (2020). New Study Suggests Smiling Influences How You See the World. Obtained from PsychologyToday: https://www.psychologytoday.com/us/blog/the-right-mindset/202008/new-study-suggests-smiling-influences-how-you-see-the-world

Sharlemann, J. et. Al. (2001) The value of a smile: Game theory with a human face. Journal of Economic Psychology; 22(5): 617–640. doi:10.1016/s0167-4870(01)00059-9.

Ueno, H., & Ives, M. (2023). Japón deja los cubrebocas y la entrenadora de sonrisas tiene mucho trabajo. Obtained from The New York Times: https://www.nytimes.com/es/2023/05/28/espanol/japon-clases-para-sonreir.html

Winkielman, P., Berridge, K. C., & Wilbarger, J. L. (2005). Unconscious Affective Reactions to Masked Happy Versus Angry Faces Influence Consumption Behavior and Judgments of Value. Personality and Social Psychology Bulletin, 31(1), 121-135. DOI:10.1177/0146167204271309.

ABOUT THE AUTHOR

 Dr. Janet Mitchell earned her dental surgery degree from the University of Panama, dedicating herself to general dentistry for several years before her passion for the field led her to pursue a Master's in Orthodontics.

In addition to being an orthodontist, Dr. Mitchell holds a bachelor's degree in Business Administration. She is the creator of the podcast "Activa tu Sonrisa" and provides care and well-being to her patients in her private practice.

Apart from her clinical work, Dr. Mitchell also finds satisfaction in teaching as a faculty member at the Interamerican University of Panama, where she shares her experience with students in the Master's program in Orthodontics. Additionally, she extends her teaching capabilities at The University of the West Indies, Jamaica, contributing to the training of future dentists by sharing her experiences and knowledge.

Beyond her dedication to dentistry, Dr. Mitchell values the time she spends with her family and friends. She recognizes the importance of a healthy work-life balance and finds joy in activities such as reading, running, and attending musical concerts.

READER'S NOTES

READER'S NOTES

READER'S NOTES

Activate Your Smile

Learn more at www.activatusonrisa.com

Contact at janet@activatusonrisa.com

Made in the USA
Coppell, TX
13 March 2024

30078471R00059